Just the Facts

Marijuana

Sean Connolly

Heinemann Library
Chicago, Illinois

Customer Service 888-454-2279
Visit our website at www.heinemannlibrary.com

Designed by M2 Graphic Design
Originated by Ambassador Litho
Printed in Hong Kong by South China Printers

07 06 05 04 03
10 9 8 7 6 5 4 3 2 1

Library of Congress Cataloging-in-Publication Data
Connolly, Sean, 1956-
  Marijuana / Sean Connolly.
    p. cm. -- (Just the facts)
Includes bibliographical references and index.
Summary: Provides an overview of the issues surrounding the use of
marijuana and the marijuana industry.
  ISBN 1-58810-680-2
  1. Marijuana abuse--Juvenile literature. 2. Marijuana
industry--Juvenile literature. 3. Marijuana--Juvenile literature. 4.
Substance abuse--Prevention--Juvenile literature. [1. Marijuana. 2. Drug
abuse.] I. Title. II. Series.
  HV5822.M3 C644 2002
  362.29'5--dc21

MAR 28 2003

2001006073

Acknowledgments
The author and publishers are grateful to the following for permission to reproduce copyright material: pp. 5,
11, 36, 40 Science Photo Library; pp. 6, 7, 21, 22, 23, 24, 26, 34, 42, 47 Corbis; pp. 8, 48 Corbis Stock
Market; pp. 12, 27, 29 Photofusion; pp. 13, 38 Popperfotto; p. 15 Network; pp. 17, 25, 39 Rex Features;
p. 18 Ancient Art and Architecture Collection; p. 19 Werner Forman; pp. 28, 33, 45 Stone; pp. 30, 31 David
Hoffman; p. 32 GettyOne; pp. 41, 44, 50 Imagebank.
Cover photographs by Janine Wiedel Photo Library and Tudor Photography.

Every effort has been made to contact copyright holders of any material reproduced in this book. Any
omissions will be rectified in subsequent printings if notice is given to the publisher.

Some words are shown in bold, **like this.** You can find out what they mean by looking in the glossary.

Contents

Marijuana

Marijuana is the most widely used illegal drug in the world. Like alcohol, it has been around for thousands of years, but the Western world has only been exposed to it in large quantities for the last 50 years or so. Even in that relatively short period, marijuana use has grown rapidly. Its users come from all walks of life and represent nearly every age group.

Obvious questions

With so many people using marijuana, society needs to know the answers to many questions about it, including what effects it has in the short term and over time. In a nutshell, the questions boil down to a single one: Is marijuana dangerous? Scientists have been trying to answer this question for some time, and a number of things seem clear. Marijuana, like any mind-altering drug, makes it hard for people to make accurate decisions—when driving, operating machinery, or even walking near traffic. Smoking marijuana is far more harmful than smoking tobacco because marijuana contains many more chemicals that damage the lungs.

Even more worrying are the **psychological** effects of using marijuana, particularly over long periods. While **high,** people often feel moody and even begin to have horrible fears that the world is "out to get them." Over time, regular users can develop a need for the drug, usually described as psychological **dependence.** For these people, going without marijuana makes them irritable, restless, and fearful. Regular marijuana use seems to make people want to escape from reality, hiding behind the changed mood created by the high. Many regular marijuana users lose interest in making new friends and trying new hobbies or interests.

Understanding the law

Some people view marijuana as relatively harmless, and argue that it should be decriminalized—the legal penalties against it should be lessened. Others even say that it should be legalized—removing all penalties for having or selling it. However, marijuana remains illegal precisely because governments need to look after the interests of the people. They believe it is in the interest of the people not to be exposed to a drug that could do them harm, even if we are, as yet, unsure about the extent of that harm. It is hardly surprising that the medical world remains concerned about a drug of which the primary effect is to distort the way people think and feel.

Marijuana leaf is rolled, like tobacco, into cigarettes known as joints or spliffs.

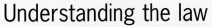

5

What Is Marijuana?

Most people learn about marijuana by word of mouth, relying on hearsay and rumor to learn about the drug and its effects. This way of passing on information distorts the truth about marijuana, and inaccuracies become greater with each retelling. Also, since the person passing on the information is often trying to persuade someone else to try marijuana for the first time (or perhaps trying to sell it), there are often exaggerations and boastful claims about its effects or harmlessness.

The marijuana plant

The term marijuana, used throughout this book, refers to a group of mind-altering products that derive from a bushy plant which grows from 3 to 18 feet (1 to 6 meters) tall. There are three **species** of marijuana plants that produce mind-altering drugs: *Cannabis sativa*, *Cannabis indica*, and *Cannabis ruderalis*. The *sativa* species has been grown for many centuries and is used to make a variety of useful products including rope, cloth, and paper. Most of these goods are produced from hemp, a strong fiber that comes from the stem of the plant. It is the leaves and flowers of this plant, as well as the *indica* and *ruderalis* species, that are dried to produce **intoxicating** effects.

Marijuana usually grows in warm places that have a great deal of sunshine. Many of the source countries for marijuana—including Colombia, Thailand, and Nigeria—are places where it grows naturally and without any real need for cultivation. Also, because hemp was a valuable item in the 19th century—it was vital in the age of sailing ships—marijuana was widely cultivated across the southern United States.

Marijuana users in North America as well as Europe are constantly trying to find new varieties that can grow in greenhouses or which have more **potency.** Some of these varieties, such as **skunk** (so named because of its distinctive foul smell) are several times stronger than ordinary marijuana.

Marijuana cultivation grew in the 19th-century golden age of sailing, since hemp was used to make ropes.

How it is taken

The dried leaves and flowers of the plant form the bulk of the illegal marijuana market around the world. People smoke this form of marijuana, either rolled in a cigarette (often called a *joint*) or in pipes, water pipes, and *bongs* (small water pipes). Some people mix the marijuana with tobacco when they roll a joint.

The other main product is **hashish,** which comes from the **resin** of the marijuana plant. This resin hardens and dealers sell it in a range of shapes, including sticky balls, chunks, or flakes. Hashish is either smoked (again, often mixed with tobacco) or cooked, in cakes and cookies, and eaten. Although already more than double the strength of ordinary marijuana, hashish can be boiled in a **solvent** such as alcohol to produce hash oil. This hash oil is usually mixed with tobacco or leaf marijuana, but sometimes smoked on its own in a pipe. It is up to 25 times as **potent** as normal marijuana and creates a quicker and more powerful **high.** Since the high is strengthened, so too are the side effects of paranoia and unease that many people feel with marijuana.

Active ingredient

Marijuana is known as a **psychoactive** drug, meaning that it affects a person's thinking. The marijuana plant contains more than 400 different chemicals, and several of these are psychoactive. The most important of these is delta-9-tetrahydrocannabinol (**THC**), which is present in the resin of the plant. Marijuana resin is concentrated in the buds of the plant, but it is also present in weaker concentrations in the leaves and stems.

The amount, or concentration, of THC in the marijuana determines its strength and the extent of the high. Ordinary marijuana, of the sort that is rolled and smoked, contains between 1 and 8 percent THC. Hashish, made from the resin itself, can have THC concentrations of up to 14 percent. Hash oil, which has had much of the non-THC material boiled away or filtered out, can have THC concentrations of 50 percent or more.

Known by many names

Marijuana and the many products made from it are known by various common terms or nicknames. Some of the terms used to describe the dried leaves include *cannabis, reefer, pot, herb, ganja, grass, dope, weed, Mary Jane,* and simply *smoke.* Hashish is often shortened to *hash* and sometimes referred to as *tar.* Hash oil is sometimes known as *oil.*

Most types of marijuana are smoked to allow the active ingredient, THC, to enter the bloodstream quickly.

How Widespread Is It?

Marijuana use around the world is widespread, and studies indicate that its use is rising. It is by far the most commonly used illegal drug.

A 1998 study of marijuana use in the United States showed that 8.3 percent of youths aged 12 to 17 were current users of the drug. Over the past 20 years, however, use within this age group has changed. The figure for the 12 to 17 year-old group reached a peak of 14.2 percent in 1979, declined to 3.4 percent in 1992, more than doubled from 1992 to 1995 (8.2 percent), and has gone up and down since then.

According to 2002 statistics from the U.S. Drug Enforcement Agency, an estimated 5 percent (11.5 million) of the U.S. population aged twelve and older were monthly marijuana or **hashish** users, which is the same rate as in 1991—but considerably lower than the rate of 13.2 percent in 1979. A similar survey found that the number of first-time marijuana users (2.3 million) had increased significantly compared to 1989 (1.4 million). At least one-third of the U.S. population has used marijuana sometime in their lives.

Drug Use Elsewhere

In 2000, the European Monitoring Center for Drugs and Drug Addiction published a report indicating that 45 million Europeans use marijuana regularly. A British survey, carried out around the same time, showed that one in ten people in England and Wales had used marijuana in the past year.

Detailed surveys carried out by Britain's Institute for the Study of Drug **Dependence** (ISDD) suggest that marijuana use hits its peak among the young. These surveys indicated that more than 1 in 3 people in the 16 to 19 year-old range (about 35 percent) had used marijuana at least once, about 30 percent had used it in the past year, and 18 percent had used it in the last month.

The Australian **Illicit** Drug Report of 2000 also showed that marijuana use among the young was widespread—and probably rising. Despite forming a National Illicit Drugs Strategy, Australia has seen illicit drug use actually rise in the past five years. Not all of this drug use is marijuana, of course, but the most recent studies indicate that 40 percent of the population over 14 years of age has tried marijuana at least once.

Regular marijuana users have a range of equipment to make cigarette rolling easier.

Voices of protest

Some people who are currently in positions of power and influence have become involved in campaigns to legalize marijuana, or at least to have it decriminalized. In some cases, these people have used the drug in the past and believe that it did them no harm. It is this view—that marijuana is basically harmless—that lies behind all their arguments. Legalizing marijuana would remove all legal controls against having or selling it. Marijuana would then be treated like alcohol or tobacco.

Decriminalizing marijuana would not go quite so far. It would still be considered illegal to sell and have large quantities, but people selling or possessing small amounts would not be arrested. They might have to pay a small fine, but there would be no permanent police record that they had committed a crime. The people who want to decriminalize marijuana believe that making marijuana legal—or almost legal— would help society in general. The police would be able to concentrate on "more important" activities such as violent crime. The government would earn money from taxes paid on marijuana, and those who need marijuana for medical reasons (see pages 26–27) would have access to supplies.

Several national organizations in the United States are fighting for changes in the marijuana laws. One of the leading groups is the National Organization for the Reform of Marijuana Laws (NORML).

People might use marijuana during all-night parties (left). Others who favor decriminalization (above) mount organized public demonstrations.

Is Marijuana Addictive?

Although the terms **addictive** and **addict** are often used in relation to drugs, most medical professionals prefer the terms *dependent* and *dependent user.* Part of the reason for this slight change of terms has to do with social matters: The word *addictive* carries a sense of being uncontrollable and even unforgivable. *Dependent,* on the other hand, suggests a type of behavior that can be overcome. Professionals also find it useful to talk of someone being either physically dependent or **psychologically** dependent on a drug.

A drug is said to cause physical **dependence** if the user continually needs to increase the dose to maintain the effects of the drug—a pattern called **tolerance**—and then suffers **withdrawal** symptoms when it is stopped. Alcohol and heroin are good examples of drugs that cause physical dependence. Psychological dependence has to do with the mind's need for the drug to cope with stress or difficult situations. Alcohol also produces a psychological dependence, as do cocaine and amphetamines.

The case of marijuana

The question of whether marijuana produces dependence has been one of the main reasons why scientists have studied it so closely. Many of these studies have been organized or monitored by the National Institute on Drug Abuse (NIDA). In a recent report, former NIDA director Dr. Charles Schuster pointed out that regular marijuana use does produce dependence —both physical and psychological.

One of the main signs that someone is dependent on a drug is how they behave when they cannot have it. Dr. Schuster found that many regular marijuana users stopped eating properly, became anxious and depressed, lost sleep, and even began to shake when their supply was stopped suddenly. These are classic signs of withdrawal, a feature of physical dependence.

Psychologically, people also show a need to continue to use marijuana if they have become regular users. These users become sluggish and withdrawn, unwilling to make decisions or even to show much enthusiasm about anything. "Younger users lose interest in school, sports, and clubs," says Dr. Schuster. Their lives seem to narrow in focus as they concentrate simply on getting and using drugs.

Drug rehabilitation centers regularly deal with people who are concerned about their marijuana use.

Evidence of the users

Most regular users would not publicly admit that they are **dependent** in any way on marijuana. It is part of the image of marijuana that people can cope, remaining "cool" and detached from everyday cares. Sometimes this view is echoed by professionals. However, in private, many of these same regular users often tell a different story.

"A lot of people think it [marijuana] is not addictive," says Ron Kadden of the University of Connecticut Health Center. "Users have been told by treatment professionals and friends that they couldn't really be addicted to marijuana." Kadden adds that many people contacted him when he advertised a treatment program designed to tackle the problem of marijuana dependence. It was the users themselves who concluded that marijuana use led to dependence, and that they needed help.

The Dutch approach

The Dutch government, like other governments, is concerned about widespread drug use among the young. While they support medical efforts to identify how and if marijuana use leads to dependence, they also accept that it is difficult to stop supplies from reaching people. So the Netherlands has chosen to try to isolate the use of marijuana in order to get people to cut down on its use.

Over the past three decades, the Netherlands has adopted a tolerant approach to the use of soft drugs such as marijuana. It has decriminalized possession below a certain amount and turned a blind eye to small-scale sales in Amsterdam's "brown cafes" and elsewhere. The Dutch view this policy as a success, pointing out that hard drug dependence is falling and that the use of marijuana is actually less widespread than in other countries where it remains illegal.

❝It is important to note that these effects [of physical dependence] occur after only a few weeks of constant use and at dosages that would be common among street users.❞

(Dr. Charles Schuster, former director of the National Institute on Drug Abuse)

The Dutch allow people to smoke limited amounts of marijuana in Amsterdam's *brown cafes.*

The Roots of the "Weed"

Marijuana cultivation and use go back thousands of years in human history, even if it has not been used to get **high** throughout that time. Scientists believe that the wild version of the *Cannabis sativa* plant originated in Central Asia. **Nomadic** people took the plant and its seeds and spread it farther afield, especially in East and South Asia. In these settings, with heavy rainfall and long hours of sunshine, the marijuana plant thrived and grew in the wild. It is likely that at this time cannabis was seen mainly as a source of useful fibers, although the lack of written records from this period—more than 5,000 years ago—leaves many gaps in our knowledge.

It is certain, though, that the Chinese soon recognized the strength and durability of the hemp fibers. They sowed seeds close together in order to produce long-stemmed plants. The hemp twines enabled the Chinese to produce strong fishing nets, stout ropes, and long-wearing mats. It is also from this time that the first recorded medical use of marijuana can be found. Marijuana is included in a list of medicines compiled for the Chinese Emperor Shen Nung around 2727 B.C.E.

Spreading the "cure"

During this period, the Chinese were beginning to use other parts of the marijuana plant besides the hemp-producing stems. They made cooking oil from the extracted seeds, and this oil was also used as a herbal remedy for cramps and fever. News of the healing properties of marijuana spread into India some time after 2000 B.C.E., and the plant was introduced by new settlers there at that time. The Indians used marijuana for a wide range of medical treatments.

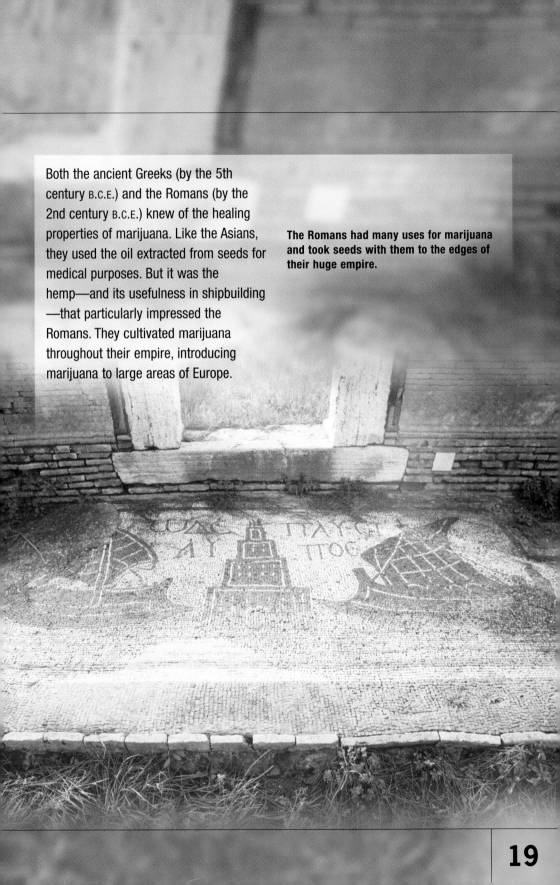

Both the ancient Greeks (by the 5th century B.C.E.) and the Romans (by the 2nd century B.C.E.) knew of the healing properties of marijuana. Like the Asians, they used the oil extracted from seeds for medical purposes. But it was the hemp—and its usefulness in shipbuilding—that particularly impressed the Romans. They cultivated marijuana throughout their empire, introducing marijuana to large areas of Europe.

The Romans had many uses for marijuana and took seeds with them to the edges of their huge empire.

Rampant Growth

From about 1500 onwards, Europeans began to take more interest in marijuana. This was the beginning of the great age of exploration and maritime trade, so demand for hemp to make rope and canvas sails grew rapidly. The word *canvas* is said to come from a Dutch pronunciation of the Greek word *cannabis*. At the same time, people began to look for different types of natural cures for illnesses. **Herbalists** re-examined ancient Greek and Roman medical records and began to spread the word about the properties of marijuana.

Rise and fall

One of the most famous 17th-century herbalists, Nicholas Culpepper of England, claimed that marijuana could be used to treat swellings, aches and pains, and even to combat **parasites.** European settlers took marijuana plants with them to the Americas, where the dual purpose of the plant—industrial and medical—continued to be appreciated. George Washington grew the plant at his Mount Vernon home. Historians looking at his diaries suggest that he set aside the potent female plants for his own medicinal use. Moreover, in the 18th and 19th centuries, people became more interested in science and technology. The **Scientific Revolution,** which spread through Europe and beyond in the 18th and 19th centuries, cast doubts on established folk remedies. Many herbal preparations (which are only now being rediscovered) were discredited and linked to medieval superstition.

Exotic influences

Although marijuana fell from favor as a medicinal aid in Europe, it remained commonly used in Asia and the Middle East. Many European travelers to Arab lands, especially soldiers in Napoleon's military campaigns, experimented with marijuana. They took the practice home with them. Beginning in France, marijuana (especially in the form of **hashish**) became popular among artists, writers, and others who styled themselves as **bohemians.** By the 1850s, the trend had gained momentum and the *Club des Haschischins* (Hashish-users Club) was formed in Paris. Its members included the great writers Dumas, Baudelaire, Flaubert, and Balzac.

Gustave Flaubert (1821–80) was a French novelist and a member of the *Club des Haschischins*.

The Modern Scene

The roots of the modern use of marijuana—with users from most elements of society—can be traced to the arts, if not necessarily the *Club des Haschischins* and its European counterparts. Artists and writers in most societies used marijuana, but the real rise came with the constantly moving population within the United States. It was at the beginning of the 20th century that the United States really began to develop. New people arrived from around the world in search of jobs. Americans themselves also began to move to new areas within their own large country. These newcomers, whether foreign or American-born, tended to move to cities, where many of them first came across marijuana.

Marijuana became even more popular among the city populations after World War I (1914–18) because the government in the United States **outlawed** alcoholic drinks in a law known as **Prohibition.** Jazz musicians used marijuana regularly, and the authorities became concerned that this spreading use would lead to a crime wave—marijuana was linked to violence and criminal behavior. In 1936, two respected magazines, *Popular Science Monthly* and *Scientific American*, published long pieces condemning marijuana as a menace to American society. By the end of the decade, every state had passed laws against its use.

Films such as the 1936 *Reefer Madness* painted a sometimes-exaggerated picture of the threat posed by marijuana.

Youth culture

Marijuana remained a hidden part of society in the United States, Britain, Australia, and many other countries for several decades. The decades immediately after World War II (1939–45), however, saw the real boom in its use. Young people became more aware of drugs, and now they could afford them. Writers such as Jack Kerouac wrote of their experiences with marijuana in the 1950s, and many young readers followed his example. By the early 1960s, people were finding it easier to get marijuana, and a new wave of rock musicians referred to it constantly in their songs.

Because marijuana was seen as a less risky **high** than that of other drugs, it gained an unofficial acceptance among many people who would not consider using anything stronger. Since its breakthrough in the 1960s, marijuana has remained a constant, retaining its popularity while other drugs—such as cocaine and ecstasy—capture the public eye for a while but come and go in and out of fashion.

Bob Marley, Jamaica's legendary reggae musician, was a regular user of marijuana.

Who Uses Marijuana?

Many drugs are associated with a particular group within society, who might be termed *high risk* and at whom drug-awareness campaigns might be targeted. For example, a large proportion of heroin and crack cocaine users come from poor, inner-city environments. Anabolic steroids are linked to athletes and people who have hobbies involving muscle building and weight training. Marijuana, however, is different. Like alcohol and tobacco, it is used in such quantity that it is impossible to give a profile of a typical user. Nevertheless, there are some trends within its pattern of use.

Starting young

In common with alcohol and tobacco, marijuana attracts young people as first-time users. Teenage users remain the most frequent users of marijuana, a figure that seems to be common in most countries (see page 10).

Many of the factors that lead young people to try alcohol and tobacco are also at work with marijuana. One of the most important is peer pressure, the feeling that someone will be considered not "cool" or daring if he or she does not try it. This pressure is tied in with the sense that most people's parents will not approve, and the sense of daring increases because marijuana is not just frowned upon, but also illegal. Just as a young drinker or smoker has probably never met someone who lost a job because of **alcoholism** or developed lung cancer because of smoking, a young marijuana user is unlikely to meet former users who felt that their lives had become worse because of marijuana.

Unspoken approval?

Of course, young people are not the only people who use marijuana. Many older people, who perhaps first used marijuana in their teens, continue to smoke the occasional joint or turn a blind eye if someone else does at a party. Young people pick up on these signals and interpret them as a green light to use marijuana themselves. When it becomes apparent that people with power and influence are trying to change society's ideas about marijuana (see page 12), the signals that a young person receives can become mixed.

"They used to show off at school—the boys mostly. 'I smoked marijuana last night, I was buzzing'—lots of showing off."

(Lisa, 18, quoted in *Drugs Wise*)

Young people begin using marijuana early in a setting where adults are regular smokers themselves.

Medicinal Uses

One of the most important—and hotly debated—issues surrounding marijuana is whether it has any real medical benefit. Any drug that can be proven to reduce pain, or make life easier for ailing patients, is welcomed by society. In the case of marijuana, though, the position becomes trickier. Many of those who want it legalized for **recreational** use believe that the first step is to persuade people that it is beneficial to health. As a result, studies that do make this suggestion are sometimes seen as being part of the pro-marijuana campaign, rather than **impartial** scientific work.

Some pro-marijuana campaigners argue that marijuana can lessen the pain and nausea that many people experience in chemotherapy.

Long history

Until around 1900, marijuana was used widely to stimulate the appetite, to relax muscles, and to combat pain. From that point on, though, this use declined as other drugs became widely available. Any further medical research stopped in the 1930s; the Marijuana Tax Act of 1937 in the United States was the most important **legislation** to curb any additional study of marijuana.

With the increased use of marijuana in the 1960s, stories began circulating about how marijuana users were gaining relief from a number of medical conditions. Three of the most common conditions mentioned were glaucoma (an eye illness), multiple sclerosis (which affects the muscles), and the nausea produced by

chemotherapy treatment against cancer. In the case of the first two, marijuana seemed to reduce pressure in the eyes and muscular stiffness. Because even the medical use of marijuana is severely limited, or even illegal, it is hard for medical science to make a definitive judgement on how effective marijuana (or **THC**) really is.

Keeping it illegal

Not everyone is convinced, however, that widening the availability of marijuana via medical use is a good idea. The California Narcotics Officers' Association, a fierce opponent of loosening marijuana laws, makes its position quite clear:

"Common sense dictates that it is not good medical practice to allow a substance to be used as a medicine if that product is:

- not Food and Drug Administration (FDA) approved
- made up of hundreds of different chemicals
- not subject to product liability regulations
- exempt from quality control standards
- not governed by recommended daily doses
- offered in unknown strengths (THC) from 1 to 10+ percent
- taken by the patient himself or herself."

Many multiple sclerosis patients say that marijuana relaxes muscles that have become stiff as a result of this disease.

The Effects of Marijuana

Like so many other aspects of marijuana, the experience and sensations that it produces are varied and hard to describe fully. Many marijuana users do not even feel any different—and certainly not **high**—the first few times that they try it. Even for those who use marijuana regularly, the effects can vary according to the person's mood or depending on the strength and type of the marijuana itself.

Laid back

People take marijuana in order to achieve a sense of relaxation, the comfortable feeling that is often described as being "laid back." It begins a few minutes after smoking the marijuana. Coupled with this sense of relaxation is a heightening of the senses: Sights, sounds, and tastes seem to become more vivid. Something that the person might normally find slightly funny becomes hilarious when the person is high.

This sense of relaxation also plays tricks with concentration, short-term memory, and the person's sense of time. People who are high often begin long sentences, only to forget how the sentence was meant to end. The passage of time seems to be slowed, and people sometimes use the term *pot time* to describe the way brief events seemed to stretch on and on. The high lasts for two to three hours, near the end of which people often become suddenly hungry (this feeling is termed the *munchies*).

Unpleasant shocks

Some people feel an acute sense of anxiety after they have smoked marijuana. Sometimes this unsettling feeling occurs even after the first puff, and it can border on **paranoia.** It is at this point that people believe that everyone is looking at them, judging them, and talking about them when they are looking away.

The sensation known as the *munchies* leaves marijuana users craving a quick food fix, often in the form of late-night fast food.

Not everyone feels this anxiety, but even the so-called "pleasant" effects of being high can be uncomfortable. People lose track of time and their memory seems faulty. They lose coordination and lose **inhibitions**—sometimes having sex when they would not normally consider it. In addition, they have several physical changes: increased heart rate, bloodshot eyes, and a dry mouth or throat. Over the longer term, regular users risk developing psychological **dependence** on marijuana as well as a number of medical complications. The most alarming of these are cancer (from smoking) and **infertility.** Both men and women reduce their ability to have children.

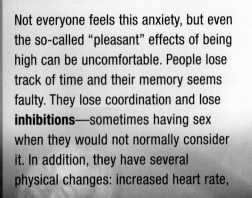

Time seems to slow down when people are high, so that even a small action—such as rolling a joint—seems to take all their attention.

How Does Marijuana Work?

Marijuana takes effect when its active chemical ingredient, **THC,** reaches the brain. How much THC reaches the brain —and how long it takes to get there— depends mainly on how the person has taken the marijuana and also on the **potency** (percentage of THC) of the marijuana itself. Marijuana is usually smoked, and the rich supply of blood in the lungs absorbs THC. Blood from the lungs goes first to the heart and then to the brain, so the **high**—as well as some other side effects—can occur within minutes. These side effects include increased heart rate and blood pressure, and the tell-tale bloodshot eyes of the user.

Eating marijuana produces the same effects, but the process takes longer because the blood has longer to travel; also, the liver breaks down some of the THC along the way. The high, as well as the side effects, develop more slowly and can take up to 90 minutes.

Inside the brain

Once it has reached the brain, the THC forms **chemical bonds** with special **receptors** using **compounds** that are already present in the brain. Alcohol and heroin work in a similar way, at least in terms of bonding with receptors in the brain. The receptors that deal with THC are located in the hippocampus, the region of the brain that is crucially involved in the formation of new memories. This fact is significant because one of the most common negative side effects of marijuana—both short-term and long-term—concerns memory loss and the inability to hold on to recently acquired knowledge.

The rush of THC into the brain is achieved quickly when marijuana is smoked from a water pipe.

Craving more?

Marijuana also bonds with receptors in other parts of the brain, in regions that deal with coordination and fine movement (other areas that are often affected during a high). The brain stem (which regulates breathing), however, remains unaffected, which means that it is impossible to suffer a fatal overdose of marijuana. The most dramatic, and as yet not fully conclusive, evidence concerns **dopamines.** Scientists know that heroin, certain other drugs (including alcohol), and even some foods release a messenger called dopamine that rushes a pleasure message through the brain. The brain remembers the pleasure and works to repeat it. Recent experiments dealing with THC indicate that the drug might also activate dopamine. If so, then it would prove that marijuana leads to **dependence.**

Marijuana smoking becomes a way of life for some users, as one joint leads to another. The brain equates the drug with pleasure, and programs the body to take in more.

Availability of Marijuana

One of the reasons underlying the widespread use of marijuana is how easy it is to obtain the drug. Before the 1970s, most marijuana used in the United States, the United Kingdom, and Australia was imported. Most of the supplies in the United States came overland from South and Central America and through Mexico. North African and Asian supplies went to European and Australian markets. All of these trade routes still exist, although the home-grown industry in most consumer countries also accounts for a rising proportion of marijuana that is sold.

Making the deal

In the United States, people might pay $200 or more for an ounce of marijuana in leaf form. **Resin** sells for about $300 for an ounce, the higher price reflecting the greater amount of **THC.** Prices rise and fall according to available supplies. If there is a shortage (perhaps caused by a large police seizure of imported marijuana), the price increases.

Home-grown marijuana, which plays an increasing role in the overall market (partly because there is less risk of being caught by customs officials), has kept prices more or less level for more than a decade. As imported supplies dry up temporarily, home-produced supplies fill the gap and hold the price steady.

Because there is so much marijuana around, coming from various suppliers, the arrangements for buying and selling it are less rigid than those governing the sale of cocaine, LSD, heroin, or other drugs. Some dealers sell only marijuana because they draw a distinction between it and other, more obviously harmful, drugs.

Marijuana, in leaf form, is usually sold in air-tight bags.

Targeting youth

This loose network means that marijuana is relatively easy to buy. Despite the zero tolerance approach of many school systems in the United States, many targeted buyers are students. First-time users of marijuana are often in junior high. A 1998 study by the U.S. National Center on Addiction and Substance Abuse indicates that adolescents are first exposed to, and try, marijuana at a very young age. According to the study, 50 percent of 13-year-olds reported that they could find and purchase marijuana, and 49 percent of teens surveyed said that they first tried it at the age of 13 or even younger.

Marijuana deals are usually made at parties and clubs where young people gather.

The Marijuana Industry

The traditional marijuana industry was based on production in certain regions (South and Central America, North Africa and Southeast Asia) and exports into consumer countries in North America, Europe, and Australia. Because most forms of marijuana (apart from **resin**) take up a great deal of space, comparatively little is smuggled into countries in aircraft luggage. Instead, importers use trucks and ships to move supplies around.

Drug trafficking organizations operating from Mexico are responsible for supplying most of the foreign marijuana available in the United States. Virtually all marijuana is smuggled into the United States concealed in false compartments, fuel tanks, seats, and tires of private and commercial vehicles. Larger shipments are usually smuggled in tractor-trailer trucks in false compartments and among everyday bulk shipments, such as agricultural products. With increased law enforcement pressure along the southwest border of the United States, marijuana smugglers are shifting to traditional routes in the Gulf of Mexico and the Bahamas. They use cargo vessels, pleasure boats, and fishing boats to sail up the coast of Mexico, either to U.S. ports or drop-off sites along the U.S. coast and the Bahamas.

Overland routes into Britain have used Spain and the Netherlands as gateways. Boats carrying marijuana to Britain and Australia avoid busy shipping lanes and head for more remote coastal waters, where the marijuana is unloaded at night onto smaller boats. The amounts of money involved in all this trade are enormous.

Home-grown and new varieties

Marijuana grows like a weed in countries with warm, sunny climates. It needs little fertilizer in these conditions, and prolonged sunshine produces **THC**-rich buds. It is not surprising that many marijuana users in California, Australia, and South Africa are able to grow their own supplies. These constitute the cheapest, and most easily produced, home-grown marijuana. In certain areas —notably remote parts of California— home-grown marijuana far exceeds the amounts needed for the personal use of the growers. A substantial **black market** has developed in these regions, and they become exporters to parts of the country with less favorable growing conditions.

U.S. customs officials, shown here along the Mexican border, are constantly on the alert for large-scale shipments of marijuana into the country.

To stop the spread of marijuana cultivation, the United States Drug Enforcement Agency (DEA) launched the Domestic Marijuana Eradication and Suppression Program in 1979; it is the only program in the United States aimed solely at marijuana. It began operations in Hawaii and California, and rapidly expanded to include all 50 states by 1985.

With the success of DEA efforts to root out marijuana plantations, many marijuana growers in the United States are moving indoors. They have begun growing new strains that are stronger and can be harvested year-round. The average **THC** content of U.S.-produced *sinsemilla* (female cannabis) rose from 3.2 percent in 1977 to 13.1 percent in 2000. Indoor growing operations range from several plants grown in a cupboard or closet to thousands of plants grown in elaborate, specially constructed greenhouses. In 2000, the five leading states for indoor growing activity were California, Florida, Oregon, Alaska, and Kentucky.

Unlike vast wooded areas where marijuana plants could go virtually undetected, Northern Europe is densely populated and lacks such protective forest cover. Moreover, the unsettled climate would not suit wide-scale cultivation of marijuana. As a result, it is in the interest of this European home-grown (and greenhouse-dependent) sector to produce the highest-grade marijuana in the smallest area.

The Dutch, who are famous for their gardening skills, have taken advantage of their country's relatively liberal marijuana laws. Dutch growers have led the way in producing many high-**potency** strains in greenhouses. Some Dutch companies openly advertise marijuana seeds for sale and export, boasting about award-winning strains. **Skunk,** the high-concentration marijuana that gets its nickname because of its distinctive strong smell, is one such variety.

Home-grown marijuana thrives with basic care. Growers buy and sell seeds for potent strains.

Against liberalization

In the United States, many groups argue that any relaxation of the firm laws and attitudes towards marijuana should be resisted.

"It is our firm belief that any movement that liberalizes or legalizes substance abuse laws would set us back to the days of the 1970s, when we experienced this country's worst drug problem and the subsequent consequences. In the 1980s, through the combined and concerted efforts of law enforcement, prevention, and treatment professionals, illicit drug use was reduced by 50 percent. Teenagers graduating from the class of 1992 had a 50 percent less likely chance of using drugs than those who graduated in the class of 1979."

(California Narcotic Officers' Association position paper)

An Australian study in 1999 estimated that the market for marijuana was worth more than A$5 billion—more than twice the amount spent on wine.

Legal Matters

Local laws

Penalties in both the United States and Australia are decided by the states themselves and can vary greatly. The penalty for possessing a small amount of marijuana in Texas, for example, is up to 180 days in prison and/or a fine of $2,000. Sentences and fines increase with the amount found and can reach 99 years in prison and a fine of $50,000. Texas law is even harsher on those who sell, especially to young people. If someone is selling marijuana within 1,000 feet (300 meters) of a school or 300 feet (90 meters) of a youth center, public pool, or video arcade, the penalty (already up to 99 years and $100,000) doubles.

Currently, in the United Kingdom, marijuana is classified as a Class B drug. However, the matter is under review. Police can issue someone caught in possession of it with either a formal warning or a formal caution. Both of these are put on police files—the warning is recorded locally and the caution goes on a national police record. Having a warning or caution on these records can affect future offenses. Depending on the amount found—or whether the person has either a warning or caution already—the police can then charge that person. The maximum penalty for possession is two years in prison and/or a fine. For intent to supply, it is five years in prison and/or a fine.

In South Australia, Australian Capital Territory, and Northern Territory, minor possession and growing offenses have been decriminalized, that is, offenders pay a fine and no conviction is recorded. In Victoria, first-time minor marijuana offenders are cautioned and referred to a drug education service. Federal law (enforced in customs cases, for example) is much harsher.

Zero tolerance

States have a great deal of independence in deciding on laws governing the possession and sale of marijuana, but local school authorities are able to impose far stricter controls on pupils. Since the 1990s, most schools in the United States have adopted a policy of *zero tolerance*, which immediately penalizes (usually through expulsion) pupils for serious offenses.

Possession and sale of marijuana is one of these serious offenses. For example, Texas schools operate their policy of zero tolerance under the guidance of a state law known as the "Safe Schools Chapter." Its wording is clear: "Students who sell, give, deliver, possess, use, or are under the influence of drugs, alcoholic beverages, or abusable chemicals must be expelled."

Customs officials target cargo ships (left) in their hunt for marijuana, but the police often stop individuals (below) to make their arrests.

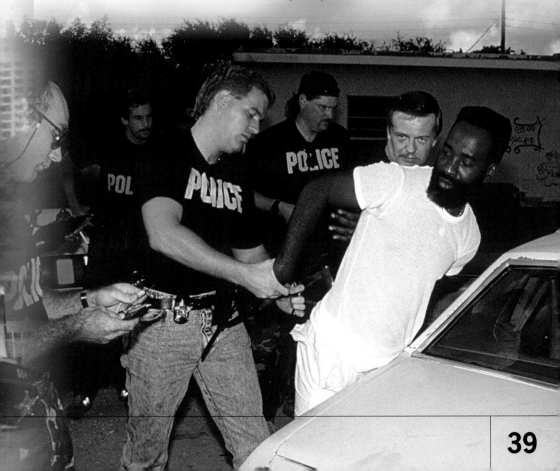

Life with Marijuana

Deception plays a large part in the lives of most drug users, and the same holds true with those who are regularly involved with marijuana. Many marijuana users believe that their behavior is harmless. They point to the poor health and reduced mental performance of those who are hooked on heroin or **dependent** on alcohol. As a result, they conclude that marijuana has none of those ill-effects. The truth is more complicated and more serious.

Being **high** on marijuana does affect someone's decision-making ability, and this change can have profound consequences. For example, someone who is high might have the same reflex speed as usual when driving, but he or she could well have difficulty concentrating on the road. The same holds true with any activity that combines physical coordination with concentration, and the results could be deadly.

Effects in the longer term

Smoking anything over a long period increases a person's risk of suffering from **respiratory** diseases, including lung cancer. Prolonged marijuana use also almost certainly leads to changes in a person's character and behavior, although it remains difficult to measure these changes. True scientific experiments (which can produce such conclusions) rely on a *control*, or a subject who does not take, for example, a drug while someone else does. There is no way that someone can lead two lives at the same time—one using marijuana regularly and the other not taking it—so the conclusions are based on what is called **anecdotal** evidence. This evidence, however, is consistent and persuasive.

The tricks marijuana plays on the mind make driving dangerous for anyone who is high.

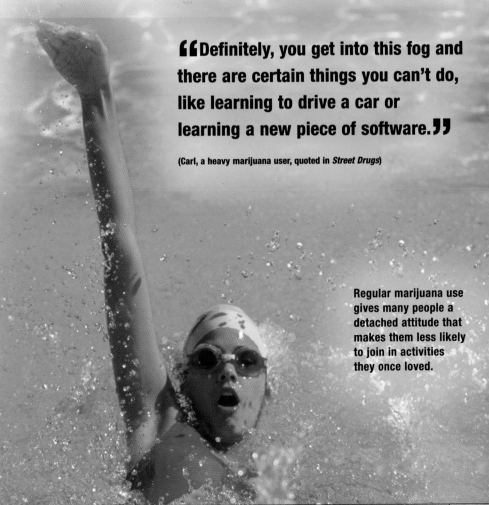

Some people argue that the disruption of the memory (which certainly occurs when someone is high) can become permanent. This is hard to prove, but a more general conclusion does seem to hold—that prolonged marijuana use can **demotivate** people. Becoming temporarily laid back is one thing, but to throw away educational or career opportunities is far more serious. Drug counselors are very concerned that teenagers, whose futures depend on educational performance and important decisions, are damaging their own future prospects because of their "so what" attitude toward such concerns.

❝Definitely, you get into this fog and there are certain things you can't do, like learning to drive a car or learning a new piece of software.❞

(Carl, a heavy marijuana user, quoted in *Street Drugs*)

Regular marijuana use gives many people a detached attitude that makes them less likely to join in activities they once loved.

"Missed the boat"

Greg, in his mid-30s, is a part-time decorator who lives in a fishing village in Maine. He believes that heavy marijuana use changed his life profoundly. "I worked hard in high school and through college and was really pleased when I was accepted at a good law school. I had smoked joints from time to time with friends, but when I found out that courses in law school were pass-fail and not graded I felt that I could put my feet up a bit and enjoy life. I started smoking more dope and missing classes; everything seemed OK because I was still passing the courses."

Life with marijuana often means just that—very little interests the user apart from the drug itself.

"I didn't know many of the teachers, but that didn't seem to matter. It turns out it did. I guess it was pretty obvious what I was up to and these guys [the academic staff at the law school] weren't exactly pleased that one of their students was so obviously unmotivated—plus doing something illegal! In my final year I was hauled into the dean's office and expelled. They quoted some obscure regulation and didn't mention dope outright, but I didn't need to read between the lines. It was hard trying to explain all this to my parents, but my father was really ill and my mother was too worried about him to react much.

"That was about fifteen years ago. You could say I sort of dropped out after that, living at home, still smoking dope, and doing odd jobs. Most of my friends are married now, but I feel I've kind of missed the boat."

Genuine need?

In June 1999, the United Kingdom's Townswomen's Guild (which is not normally associated with civil protests) held their Annual General Meeting in the Royal Albert Hall in London. One of the prominent speakers was Clare Hodges from the Alliance for Cannabis Therapeutics. "I've had multiple sclerosis for seventeen years and after I'd had it for ten years I began to find that I was getting very ill and I was getting no relief from the medicines," she said. "Somebody told me about marijuana, and I tried it—I was at my wit's end."

Having listened to Ms. Hodges' personal testimony, the Guild voted overwhelmingly in favor of legalizing marijuana for medicinal purposes. They were also swayed by the testimony of several doctors who reported that marijuana provided the only relief for patients suffering from chronic pain, bladder problems, and who had difficulty in controlling muscle spasms. Both doctors and patients risk criminal prosecution for using marijuana and two patients have already been prosecuted for growing their own supplies.

❝Scientific data indicate the potential therapeutic value of cannabinoid drugs ... for pain relief, control of nausea and vomiting, and appetite stimulation. ... Except for the harms associated with smoking, the adverse effects of marijuana use are within the range tolerated for other medications.❞

(National Academy of Science, Institute of Medicine findings from a 1999 study, *Marijuana and Medicine: Assessing the Science Base*.)

Family and Friends

Some marijuana users smoke an occasional joint, perhaps over a weekend, and feel that they are still very much in control of their lives. They believe this because the signs of being **high** are less obvious than, for example, being drunk. This often makes them think that they have fooled other members of their family.

Drifting along

Although the signs of being stoned can be masked, it is less easy for a person to hide the fact that they are using marijuana regularly. Patterns of behavior do change, along with a fundamental change of attitude.

The sense of being laid back, which for many people is one of the attractions of the marijuana high, carries over into everyday life. Things that once seemed important, such as studying hard, can appear absurd, and many regular marijuana users look down on others who are caught up with the "rat race" (as they see it) of competition and hard work. Many users get high before, during, and after school, lying to their parents about what they are doing.

A family dinner can seem like a waste of time for someone who smokes marijuana regularly.

These changes in behavior also affect friendships. Regular users usually find themselves in the company of fellow users, and grow apart from old friends. Apart from the changes of attitude in the regular users is another big barrier: They are engaged in an illegal activity while their former friends are not. That barrier puts pressure on the friends, who often feel that they would be scorned if they talked to parents or teachers—even if they knew they were acting in the true spirit of friendship.

Marijuana users have a reputation for being aimless and unlikely to get excited about new activities.

❝I had never lived with the fear that I had no friends, so I did almost anything to keep the two good friends I still had. One of the things I did was try pot for the first time. This was a big change from the way I lived when I was younger. I was an athlete, and the last thing I thought I would get into was drugs. Drugs prevented me from being the best athlete I could be.❞

(Former user's account on the Marijuana Anonymous Web site)

Treatment and Counseling

When people talk about treatment and counseling, they are usually referring to the large group of drugs that lead to **dependence,** especially physical dependence. Some form of outside help—in the form of therapy sessions, substitute drugs, or one-on-one counseling—is often necessary to overcome the compulsive desire to have more of the drug. Marijuana is different. Dependence is hard to prove conclusively, although many users and former users believe that it is a definite problem. This uncertainty, ironically, can make it harder for marijuana users to face up to their problem than those who are hooked on heroin or who are problem drinkers—since both of these drugs are well-known examples of dependence drugs.

Breaking free

Regular users often deny that they have a problem, even if they spend most of their time when they aren't already **high** thinking about getting high or getting drugs. Many believe the argument that marijuana does not produce any type of dependence, physical or psychological, and this belief prevents them from seeing what effect marijuana is having on their lives.

Unlike most other drugs, including alcohol, **THC** (the active chemical in marijuana) is stored in fat cells and therefore takes longer to clear the body than any other common drug. This means that some parts of the body still retain THC even after a couple of months, rather than just the couple of days or weeks for water soluble drugs. Many people experience **psychological** or emotional symptoms such as **insomnia** and depression during this time. Then, because THC tends to dampen the dreaming mechanism in the brain, vivid—and often disturbing—dreams return. Throughout this time users can feel at the mercy of their emotions, jumping from irritation and anger to **euphoria** and back again.

Although marijuana withdrawal can never match the unsettling effects of coming off heroin or alcohol (**delirium tremens** and the shakes), many people do have physical symptoms. The most common are headaches and night sweats (sweating is one of the body's natural ways of getting rid of toxins). Many people also find that they lose their appetite for a few weeks, possibly losing weight or feeling nauseated as well. Most of these symptoms, like the psychological symptoms, are gone after two or three months.

Tackling dependence

Despite the voices that argue that marijuana does not lead to either psychological or physical dependence, many drug therapists believe that it is difficult for a regular user to cut down or stop. Many people do find that marijuana has become too important in their lives. One organization, Marijuana Anonymous (MA), offers a chance for such users to confront their own lives in a supportive atmosphere. MA is one of many organizations that model itself on Alcoholics Anonymous (AA), which has helped thousands of people overcome their dependence on alcohol.

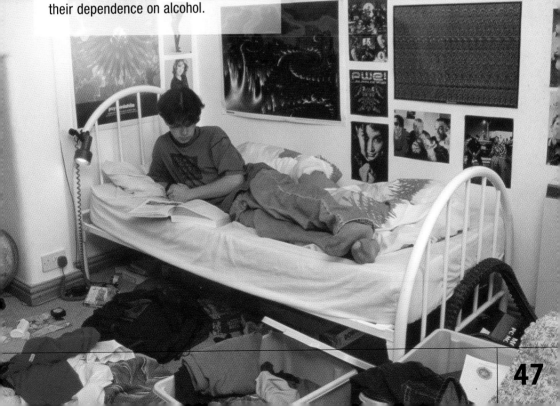

The real world can seem pale and dull without marijuana—especially if the former user lost interest in other activities while using the drug.

Following the example set by AA, Marijuana Anonymous uses the same methods (friendship, honesty, and **anonymity** in meetings) and goals (to remain free of the substance).

MA asks regular marijuana users to consider its twelve questions (see right). A "yes" answer to one or more of these questions can indicate a serious problem with marijuana. By acknowledging the problems themselves, marijuana users have taken the first (and hardest) step towards recovery. Shared experiences with other members provide a network of support and allow users to recognize that they are not alone.

"An informed citizenry... is the most effective deterrent of all."

(American Medical Association)

The twelve Marijuana Anonymous questions

1. Has smoking pot stopped being fun?
2. Do you ever get **high** alone?
3. Is it hard for you to imagine a life without marijuana?
4. Do you find that your friends are determined by your marijuana use?
5. Do you smoke marijuana to avoid dealing with your problems?
6. Do you smoke pot to cope with your feelings?
7. Does your marijuana use let you live in a privately defined world?
8. Have you ever failed to keep promises you made about cutting down or controlling your dope smoking?
9. Has your use of marijuana caused problems with memory, concentration, or motivation?
10. When your stash is nearly empty, do you feel anxious or worried about how to get more?
11. Do you plan your life around your marijuana use?
12. Have friends or relatives ever complained that your pot smoking is damaging your relationship with them?

Experienced counselors have a lot to offer
young people who might have confused ideas
about marijuana and its effects.

People to Talk To

Although marijuana use has increased dramatically over the years, the information about it can still seem incomplete and contradictory to many young people. Some of the certainties about marijuana—such as the fact that you can get a criminal record for using it, get expelled from school, or develop lung cancer in the longer term—can get distorted by word of mouth. Young people usually hear of the buzz of the **high**, the giggles, and the munchies, and never of the lethargy and lack of motivation among those who use marijuana over long periods. This type of peer pressure is not helpful, but it is a strong and persuasive force.

Other voices

There are, however, people who can put things in a different perspective, either by giving first-hand accounts of their own drug experiences or by outlining the clear dangers of any drug abuse. Parents and older family members are usually the best people to turn to first. In many cases, the parents of teenagers will have had first-hand exposure to marijuana themselves in their own youth. Nevertheless, the teenage years are often the period when young people feel that they have least in common with their parents. Even sympathetic teachers and others in authority locally might seem "too close to home."

The United States has a wide range of telephone contacts—many of them toll-free and most of them anonymous—where young people can find out more about marijuana and other drugs. Many of the organizations listed in the Information and Advice section (pages 52–53) either provide a service over the phone or they can suggest local agencies throughout the United States. Others are geared specifically to questions coming from younger people. Whether you approach one of these organizations, a family member, a youth leader, or teacher, the important thing is to be able to talk—and listen—freely about your drug concerns. Sharing a problem or worry is the first step to solving it.

Emotions are often heightened when a person is high—which is bad news if the emotion was fear or worry to begin with.

&&This first major sign of success has occurred because parents, teachers, coaches, ministers, and community coalitions are all working together in a comprehensive national and local effort. The future should show additional improvements as well. The fact that the numbers are best for the youngest (12–17) group is a [suggestion] that use will continue to fall as this group grows older.**JJ**

(White House National Drug Policy Director Barry McCaffrey, referring to the drop in teenage marijuana use in the late 1990s)

Information and Advice

The United States is well served by organizations providing advice, counseling, and other information relating to drug use. All of the contacts listed on these pages are helpful places for obtaining such advice, or for providing confidential information over the telephone or by mail.

Child Welfare League of America
440 First Street NW
Washington, DC 20001
(202) 638-2952
The Child Welfare League of America, based in Washington, provides useful contacts across the country in most areas relating to young people's problems, many of them related to drug involvement.

D.A.R.E. America
P.O. Box 775
Dumfries,VA 22026
(703) 860-3273
Drug Abuse Resistance and Education (D.A.R.E.) America is a national organization that links law-enforcement and educational resources to provide up-to-date and comprehensive information about all aspects of drug use.

Marijuana Anonymous
Web site: www.marijuana-anonymous.org
The MA Web site is a starting point for information on the organization's aims and activities, as well as comprehensive links to local branches of MA around the world.

Partnership for a Drug-Free America
405 Lexington Avenue, Suite 1601
New York, NY 10174
(212) 922-1560
The Partnership for a Drug-Free America® is a coalition of communications professionals—from advertising, the media industry, public relations, research companies, actors guilds, and production companies—dedicated to one mission: to help kids and teens reject substance abuse by influencing attitudes through persuasive information.

Youth Power
300 Lakeside Drive
Oakland, CA 94612
(510) 451-6666, ext. 24
Youth Power is a nationwide organization involved in widening awareness of drug-related problems. It sponsors clubs and local affiliates across the country in an effort to help young people make their own sensible choices about drugs, and to work against the negative effects of peer pressure.

More Books To Read

Connolly, Beth. *Through a Glass Darkly: The Psychological Effects of Marijuana and Hashish.* Broomall, Penn.: Chelsea House, 1998.

De Angelis, Therese and Judy Hasday. *Marijuana.* Broomall, Penn.: Chelsea House, 1999.

Herscovitch, Arthur. *Everything You Need to Know about Drug Abuse.* New York : Rosen Publishing Group, 2000.

Lawler, Jennifer. *Drug Legalization: A Pro/Con Issue.* Berkeley Heights, NJ: Enslow Publishers, 2000.

Masline, Shelagh Ryan. *Drug Abuse and Teens.* Berkeley Heights, NJ: Enslow Publishers, 2000.

Schleichert, Elizabeth. *Marijuana.* Berkeley Heights, NJ: Enslow Publishers, 1996.

Somdahl, Gary. *Marijuana Drug Dangers.* Berkeley Heights, NJ: Enslow Publishers, 1999.

Glossary

addict
someone who is dependent on a drug

addictive
leading to dependence, as with a drug

alcoholism
disease linked to a dependence on alcohol

anecdotal
relying on descriptions rather than scientific experiments

anonymity
ability to keep one's name secret

black market
illegal sale of products such as drugs

bohemian
not worried about the rules set down by a society

chemical bonds
strong forces that bind atoms and molecules together

chemotherapy
cancer treatment that involves giving the patient a series of strong chemicals, which leads to side effects such as fatigue and nausea

compound
substance composed of two or more elements

delirium tremens
series of nightmare-like images and shaking that occurs when someone who is dependent on alcohol goes without it

demotivate
to cause someone to lose interest in things

dependence
need or craving for a substance, especially a drug—can be either a psychological or a physical craving

dopamine
chemical substance in the brain that regulates movement and emotion

drug trafficking
illegally transporting large amounts of drugs from one country to another

euphoria
sense of profound happiness and well-being

hashish
often shortened to *hash*; a strong type of marijuana which comes from the resin of the marijuana plant

herbalist
someone who grows and understands the medicinal qualities of herbs

high
(in this sense) effect people feel after using marijuana

illicit
against the law, illegal

impartial
fair and just, not biased

infertility
inability to have children because of medical problems

inhibition
sense of caution that stops people from behaving recklessly

insomnia
inability to fall asleep or remain asleep

intoxicating
causing someone to lose physical or mental control temporarily

legislation
laws based on acts passed by a representative body such as Congress

nomadic
constantly moving around, with no permanent home

outlaw
to make illegal

paranoia
belief that everyone is "out to get you"

parasite
tiny creature such as an insect or worm that lives inside another animal

potency
strength of a chemical or drug

Prohibition
period (1919–1933) in the United States when alcoholic drinks were illegal

psychoactive
having an effect on the mind

psychological
dealing with the mind or brain

receptors
(in the human brain) organs that receive signals from the nervous system

recreational
(in terms of drugs) taking for pleasure, rather than as a medicine

resin
thick liquid containing the highest amounts of THC of any part of the marijuana plant

respiratory
relating to the lungs or breathing

Scientific Revolution
historical period, roughly from the late 1600s to the mid 1800s, when increased scientific curiosity led to many new discoveries

skunk
nickname of a particularly powerful variety of the marijuana plant

solvent
liquid that can dissolve many other substances, including chemicals that affect the human brain

species
scientific category of plants or animals. Individuals of the same species resemble each other and can only breed with others of the same species

THC
delta-9-tetrahydrocannabinol, the active chemical ingredient of marijuana

tolerance
ability of the body to absorb increasing amounts of a drug

withdrawal
difficult process of giving up a drug, and the physical and psychological effects the process creates

Index